Murder Well Rehearsed

by John R. Carroll

Single copies of plays are sold for reading purposes only. The copying or duplicating of a play, or any part of play, by hand or by any other process, is an infringement of the copyright. Such infringement will be vigorously prosecuted.

Baker's Plays
7611 Sunset Blvd.
Los Angeles, CA 90042
bakersplays.com

NOTICE

This book is offered for sale at the price quoted only on the understanding that, if any additional copies of the whole or any part are necessary for its production, such additional copies will be purchased. The attention of all purchasers is directed to the following: this work is fully protected under the copyright laws of the United States of America, the British Commonwealth, including Canada, and all other countries of the Copyright Union. Violations of the Copyright Law are punishable by fine or imprisonment, or both. The copying or duplication of this work or any part of this work, by hand or by any process, is an infringement of the copyright and will be vigorously prosecuted.

This play may not be produced by amateurs or professionals for public or private performance without first submitting application for performing rights. Licensing fees are due on all performances whether for charity or gain, or whether admission is charged or not. Since performance of this play without the payment of the licensing fee renders anybody participating liable to severe penalties imposed by the law, anybody acting in this play should be sure, before doing so, that the licensing fee has been paid. Professional rights, reading rights, radio broadcasting, television and all mechanical rights, etc. are strictly reserved. Application for performing rights should be made directly to BAKER'S PLAYS.

No one shall commit or authorize any act or omission by which the copyright of, or the right to copyright, this play may be impaired. No one shall make any changes in this play for the purpose of production.

Publication of this play does not imply availability for performance. Both amateurs and professionals considering a production are strongly advised in their own interest to apply to Baker's Plays for written permission before starting rehearsals, advertising, or booking a theatre.

Whenever the play is produced, the author's name must be carried in all publicity, advertising and programs. Also, the following notice must appear on all printed programs, "Produced by special arrangement with Baker's Plays."

Licensing fees for MURDER WELL REHEARSED are based on a per performance rate and payable one week in advance of the production.

Please consult the Baker's Plays website at www.bakersplays.com or our current print catalogue for up to date licensing fee information.

Copyright © 1976 by Walter H. Baker Company
Made in U.S.A.
All rights reserved.

MURDER WELL REHEARSED
ISBN 978-0-87440-733-4
#15710-B

STORY OF THE PLAY

As this suspense-thriller is chillingly unraveled, we find a group of performers preparing for a rehearsal only to discover a slain body center stage. Amidst sharp accusations, careless amateur attempts at crime solving and tense hysterics, steps an over confident Police Inspector. Suddenly, the stage is in blackout during which the body mysteriously disappears. In addition, all the doors to the auditorium are barred and this overwrought group is forced to the realization that they might be held captive by a crazed killer. Subsequent blackouts, total disruption of all phone service, an abrupt closing of the stage curtain and eerily pre-recorded threatening messages whip this easily staged one act into a theatre piece of enormous excitement and genuine suspense. A unique surprise ending.

CAST

NAN, a drama coach.
FRANK, a groundkeeper.
SHEILA, a student.
TOM, a student.
MEG, a student.
JIMMIE, a student.
INSPECTOR WEBB.

PLACE: A rehearsal stage.

TIME: Present.

MURDER WELL REHEARSED

SCENE: The School Auditorium at Carver High School. The Curtains are closed. As the houselights start to dim, NAN and FRANK enter from the auditorium and walk towards the stage. They carry on a conversation as if no one were there.

NAN: Thanks, Frank. I promise I'll never forget my keys again.

FRANK: What are groundkeepers for but to help absent-minded teachers into buildings after hours.

NAN: When you've been here a little longer, you'll get used to the Drama Club's late hours. (Starts to climb onto apron.)

FRANK: You sure do spend a lot of time in here. Why, the two weeks I've been working here, I've seen you more than any other faculty member. Running here, running there, you certainly do keep busy.

NAN: I want to really build this club. It takes a lot of work, but I think it'll be worth it. (Exits back stage through curtains.) A school the size of Carver should have a good Theatre Arts Club. (Opens curtain to reveal a rehearsal set — an old couch, some rehearsal chairs and a closet door.) But if we don't get this play clicking, we may fall flat on our face. (Enters)

FRANK: Trouble?

NAN: No more than usual. The set isn't done, the lights are all wrong, the costumes aren't finished, and on top of everything else, the school is talking about cutting our budget. Just the usual mayhem two weeks before another Carver production.

FRANK: They're going to cut your budget, eh? (NAN starts picking up empty pop bottles from stage.)

NAN: Well, Mr. Gleason was trying awfully hard at the last meeting. The old goat hates the Drama Club. Says it's a waste of time and money. He was anything but pleased when I was appointed Drama Coach. Thinks I'm too

MURDER WELL REHEARSED Page 6

young.

FRANK: Well, I'll be rooting for you.

NAN: Thanks, Frank. Maybe bitterness comes with the jobs here. Not too many people are on my side.

FRANK: Look, I've only been here two weeks, but I think you're doing a real good job.

NAN: Thanks. Well, I hope we don't disturb you. (Throws trash in can.)

FRANK: Naw, my house is way across the football field. You could do "Hello Dolly" with a chorus of guerrillas and I still would sleep through.

NAN: Well, this is hardly a musical. It's called "Midnight", all about a murder.

FRANK: Who done it?

NAN: You think I'm going to tell you the ending? No, sir! You won't get out of buying a ticket that easy!

FRANK: Bet it's the butler.

NAN: Don't put any money on it. (There is a loud banging on the door and we hear voices yelling) Ah, there's our murderers now. Would you get that, Frank? I'll get some more lights on. (She goes behind the curtain as FRANK goes to door and lets in SHEILA, TOM and MEG.)

SHEILA: Thanks, Frank.

MEG: Did Miss Benton forget her keys again? (MEG, TOM and SHEILA climb onto stage.)

FRANK: Right. So you're the murderers, huh?

SHEILA: I'm not. I'm assistant director.

TOM: Don't look at me. I'm the friendly cop on the beat.

FRANK: That leaves you, Miss. (Additional lights go up on stage. MEG walks center stage.)

MEG: (Evidently reciting lines from the play) "Why, Inspector, I have an iron clad alibi. On the night of the murder I was visiting my sick philodendron in the plant hospital."

TOM: (Joins her, center, using an Irish Brogue.) "Well, Missie. Now I've heard everything. Talking to a plant, is it?

SHEILA: (Laughing) I vote that Tom's the murderer.

TOM: Me?

SHEILA: Yes, you murdered that Irish accent. (All laugh.)

FRANK: Well, good luck, kids. I gotta go lock up the science lab. Goodnight, Miss Benton. (NAN re-appears.)

NAN: Goodnight, Frank. And Thanks again. (All exchange good-byes and FRANK exits.) Well, you people are all on time for a change. Where's everyone else?

TOM: Isn't Jimmy here?

NAN: No, not yet.

TOM: That's funny. We saw his van parked outside.

NAN: Well, let's start on the second scene in Act Two, he's not in that one.

TOM: I'm really having a tough time with that long speech. I just can't get it down. (They start to get ready.)

NAN: (Sits down left with a note pad and script. SHEILA exits off right.) O.K. Take your places. (TOM and MEG go onto the set and take character stances.) Lights up and start.

MEG: (Emoting) Charles, why all these questions?

TOM: Just my duty, ma'm. There's been a murder committed. I just want to get to the bottom of it.

MEG: But surely you don't think that I . . .

TOM: I'm just here to get the facts ma'm. You say that you were . . . were . . . ah . . .

NAN: (Prompting) Last seen at the club . .

TOM: Oh yeah. Last seen at the club. And yet, we have found out that the club was closed on the night in question. Is it possible that you didn't go to the club at all, but instead snuck home and killed your husband?

MEG: That's ridiculous. You know that my husband and I were . . . (She sits on the couch which is covered by a white sheet. As soon as she sits, she screams and jumps up.)

NAN: What's wrong?

MEG: There's something under this.

TOM: Jimmy! Stop horsing around.

SHEILA: (Coming from the wings.) Probably some old costumes. (They take off the sheet. SHEILA and MEG scream.)

MURDER WELL REHEARSED Page 8

TOM: It's . . . It's Mr. Gleason. (They all start talking.)

NAN: (Crosses to Mr. Gleason, examines him and pauses.) He's dead! (Pulls sheet back over Gleason.) (SHEILA and MEG starts to sob. She sits on the easy chair.)

TOM: Looks like he was hit on the head by something pretty heavy.

MEG: Who . . Who would do anything like that? (NAN goes to her.)

NAN: Come on, Meg. Calm down.

SHEILA: Shouldn't we . . . we call the police or something?

TOM: I can go and . . . (Off stage we hear a low moan. MEG and SHEILA scream, running away from noise.) What was that?

NAN: What?

TOM: That noise. (Moan is heard off again, more screams.)

MEG: (Hysterically) It's the murderer! He's going to kill us all. (The moan is closer now, additional screams.)

NAN: Tom, grab that board. I'll get the chair. (They get the board and chair and slowly walk stage left.)

SHEILA: Be careful! (The moan is heard very loudly and JIMMY staggers in, a crowbar in his hand. NAN and TOM freeze in mid swing.)

SHEILA: Jimmy! What are you doing?

JIMMY: (Groggily) I wish I could tell you. My head!

NAN: (Putting down chair) What's wrong? What happened?

JIMMY: I was hit . . . I think. (He sits on one of the rehearsal chairs, dropping the crowbar.)

NAN: (Seeing the crowbar) Who? Who hit you?

JIMMY: (Trying to remember) I came early so I could go over that speech I never can remember and the place was locked up. So I climbed in through the dressing room window. It's always unlocked. I came in and . . . and I remember hearing you guys rehearsing then, BAM! I just woke up now.

MEG: With a crowbar in your hands?

JIMMY: Yeah. Isn't that weird! O.K. Who's the clown that hit me?

NAN: What time was this, Jimmy?

JIMMY: I don't know. About six thirty, I guess.

NAN: Then that wasn't us you heard. We just got here. You didn't see anyone, did you?

JIMMY: No. Hey, what's going on? I get hit on the head, you're all cross-examining me. I feel like I'm in the third act of "Midnight".

TOM: You are. Only the murderer hasn't been revealed yet.

JIMMY: Huh? (NAN shows him the body.) What . . . what happened?

NAN: We don't know. You probably came in just as the murderer was trying to escape. Did you see anything?

JIMMY: (Staring at Gleason's body) Who would want to . . .

NAN: Jimmy, did you see anyone? (JIMMY turns, dazed, NAN re-covers Gleason.)

JIMMY: Wha . . . Oh, no. Nothing. You know how dark it is backstage with the lights off. Did you call the police?

NAN: We were just going to. I'll use the backstage phone. Everyone, just stay calm. I'll be right back. (She exits.)

TOM: I don't get it, Jimmy. You're never early.

JIMMY: I was today. Hey, what do you mean? Are you suspecting me!

TOM: No, of course not. But the police are going to be mighty suspicious. Especially since that crowbar has your fingerprints all over it.

MEG: That's right! Oh, Jimmy. I hope you have a good alibi.

JIMMY: Would you guys knock it off. You make it sound like you're rehearsing the play. I'm innocent. It's that simple. You think I go around bashing my head in?

SHEILA: We're sorry, Jimmy. It's just that everyone's a little nervous.

JIMMY: Yeah. It's all right. (NAN re-enters) Did you get the police?

NAN: The switchboard is dead. We'll have to go to a pay phone.

SHEILA: Fine!

MEG: I don't care. I just want to get out of here.

MURDER WELL REHEARSED Page 10

TOM: I'll go and call if you want.

NAN: I think we shall all go.

JIMMY: Good idea. (They all start to exit but before they get off the stage, INSPECTOR WEBB enters. He wears a trench coat and glasses.)

SHEILA: (Screaming) Who are you? (They all back up)

WEBB: Inspector Webb, homicide. There's been a murder! (He flashes them a card.)

MEG: How did you know?

WEBB: We got a call down at headquarters. An excited old lady said to come down here. Said that Mr. Gleason had been murdered.

NAN: Right over there. (Points to body. WEBB goes to it, checks it over.)

WEBB: Been hit over the head with something heavy. (He spies the crowbar and picks it up, using a handkerchief so as not to destroy the prints.) How convenient. The murderer left his weapon.

JIMMY: I think you'll find my fingerprints on that.

WEBB: Yours?

JIMMY: Yes. I was here early and someone hit me on the head. When I woke up, that was in my hand.

WEBB: Wait a minute. Let's start at the beginning. What are you people doing here?

NAN: I'm Nan Benton, Coach of the Drama Club. We came here to have a rehearsal for the school play and found Gleason dead.

WEBB: So you're Nan Benton.

NAN: Yes.

WEBB: Interesting. The old lady who called and told us about this said that you were the one who killed him.

NAN: What?

JIMMY: That's ridiculous.

SHEILA: Who was she?

WEBB: She didn't give her name. Just said there was a murder, said to find Nan Benton 'cause she did it and hung up. We thought it was a crank call but now . . . (Gestures toward body)

SHEILA: But Miss Benton got here just a few minutes before us.

WEBB: Did anyone see him? (All are silent) What about you, kid? (Points to Jimmy) Want to explain where you were?

JIMMY: I told you. I came in through the window, and someone hit me on the head. When I came to, I had that in my hand.

WEBB: Did your assailant resemble Miss Benton?

JIMMY: No! I mean, I don't know. It was too dark. But she wouldn't . . .

WEBB: So you came to rehearse and when you kids got here, Miss Benton was already in the auditorium with a dead body on the couch and a kid knocked out in the dressing rooms. Didn't it seem mighty suspicious to you?

NAN: Look, go ask Frank, the groundkeeper. He let me in tonight.

WEBB: What time?

NAN: About a quarter to seven – seven – I don't know.

WEBB: Where is this guy?

NAN: He lives in the little house across from the football field.

WEBB: So, you get here, don't notice a body lying center stage until your students get here.

NAN: That's right. I was here about ten minutes before they came.

WEBB: But the call came in about a quarter of an hour ago. Do you have any idea who could have made that call?

NAN: None. And I can't see why she'd blame me.

WEBB: Did you and Gleason have any misunderstandings?

NAN: No more than usual.

WEBB: Meaning?

TOM: Look, everyone knew Mr. Gleason didn't like the Drama Club. He resented everything we did.

JIMMY: We all had our disagreements with him. In fact, today I was . . . (He stops short)

INSPECTOR: Yes, you were about to say something.

MURDER WELL REHEARSED Page 12

JIMMY: Nothing. I mean, well, today Mr. Gleason and I were talking, that's all.

WEBB: When?

JIMMY: This afternoon. He said he felt the money for this show was just a waste of school funds. That really burned me up and . . . I mean . . . I . . . he . . .

WEBB: Upset you enough to (Picks up crowbar) do something about it?

NAN: Leave the kids alone, huh?

JIMMY: Doesn't this lump tell you something, Inspector?

WEBB: You can all tell your stories down at headquarters.

MEG: Headquarters? You mean we're all suspects?

WEBB: No. We just want your stories. I'm going to call an ambulance and a back-up squad. Don't any of you move. (He starts off)

NAN: (Calling off) The phone is . .

WEBB: I'll find it. (He is off) And don't move. I can see you all from here.

NAN: But the switchboard is . . . Oh, he'll find out.

MEG: I don't like the way he insinuates about you and Mr. Gleason, Miss Benton.

TOM: You . . . You didn't kill him, did you?

MEG: Tom! First we grill Jimmy, now Miss Benton. I think the sooner we get out of here the better for all of us.

NAN: Thanks for the vote of confidence, Tom. I can't imagine who called the police. No one knew I'd be here except for you people.

SHEILA: Don't look at me. I don't want to spend my life behind bars.

MEG: I don't even know the police phone number. I'm afraid the only number I know is "Take Out" for Sullivan's Pizza.

TOM: All you do is have to dial zero for the cops. So in that case, we're all suspects.

NAN: It doesn't add up. I get here, you arrive, Jimmy is in the dressing room unconscious. That means the murderer was still here at . . . what time?

MURDER WELL REHEARSED

JIMMY: I guess about six-thirty.

MEG: He might still be here? I want to leave!

NAN: I doubt it. After he knocked Jim out I'm sure he realized there would be more of us coming. His first thought was probably escape.

SHEILA: Your poor head, Jimmy. (She goes to rub it) Jim, you're bleeding.

JIMMY: Where? (SHEILA searches his scalp)

SHEILA: That's funny. There's spots of blood on your pants here, but I can't find where it's coming from.

TOM: (Looks at pant leg) And it's fresh, too!

MEG: I want to get out of this place.

NAN: Calm down. As soon as Webb comes back, we'll get going.

SHEILA: I don't get it. If you're not cut, Jimmy . . .

TOM: That means someone must have bled on you. Like Mr. Gleason! (They all turn and stare at Jimmy. WEBB re-enters)

JIMMY: Look, I didn't kill him, I tell you. I'd have cut out a lot sooner if I had.

WEBB: Exactly what I was thinking. Why didn't you?

JIMMY: Because I don't have any reason to leave.

WEBB: Yet, all the clues seem to say otherwise. Headquarters is sending down a couple more units to escort you back to the station. They'll bring an ambulance for your friend. I suggest we all relax here until they come.

JIMMY: Relax? How can I relax when everyone is sure I'm a murderer?

WEBB: Not everyone.

JIMMY: The real murderer.

SHEILA: You mean you believe Jimmy?

WEBB: I'm not saying. It just seems a little too pat. Why didn't he leave when he had a chance? Why not wipe off the fingerprints? It seems to me he's being set up by the real murderer.

NAN: That puts me back in prime target, doesn't it?

WEBB: You got it, Benton. You were saying earlier that

MURDER WELL REHEARSED

you didn't get along with Gleason.

SHEILA: Why are you harping on her!

TOM: (Who has been sitting in a corner thinking) Sheila, come here.

SHEILA: What do you want . . . (She goes to TOM and they talk quietly)

NAN: Keep her busy, Tom, while the Inspector has to say his little piece. All right, Inspector, why not just come out and book me? Maybe because you don't have enough evidence, huh? I tell you, find Frank. He'll verify. He was with me until my students arrived.

WEBB: Look, all I'm saying . . . (Suddenly all the lights go out, a total BLACKOUT. We hear the ad-lib voices: What's going on? What happened? Screams, etc.)

MEG: It's the murderer. He's here. I know it (Girls continue to scream. We hear movement)

NAN: Quick. Check the light board.

TOM: Ow! Someone bumped into me!

SHEILA: Where is everyone? (They continue talking all at once. Suddenly, a spotlight hits NAN, center stage. Dazed, she looks up to the source of light. We hear a distorted voice over the P.A. System)

VOICE: Confess, murderer! Confess! Your time is at hand! CONFESS! (There is a hysterical laugh as the INSPECTOR runs into the light and stares up)

WEBB: Quick, show me where the light switches are. He's there! (NAN and WEBB run off.)

JIMMY: Tom, turn on some light. (TOM exits)

MEG: Does this mean the murderer is still here?

SHEILA: I don't get it. But I think we better get out of here. (The lights go on. The spot goes off)

JIMMY: (Going to wings) Tom, did you find anything? (TOM re-enters)

TOM: Our murderer was clever. He had the lights put on a timer. He timed that blackout.

MEG: You mean he wasn't working the lights at all?

TOM: No.

SHEILA: That does it folks. Let's get out of here.
JIMMY: Look, here comes Miss Benton (NAN enters)
MEG: Did you find him?
NAN: No. The spotlight was hooked up to the timer. It was set to go off along with the lights.
SHEILA: But that voice . . .
NAN: (Holds up tape for a recording.) Don't you recognize your own props? Remember the tape we use for the final scene during the seance . . .?
SHEILA: You mean the murderer had the tape recorder hooked to the timer?
TOM: Clever. But that means the murderer must have been awfully familiar with the place and the props we have . . . (He realizes what he is saying) Look, Miss Benton, I don't suspect you, honest! I was just . . .
NAN: It's O.K., Tom. Right now I'm so confused I don't know what to think.
SHEILA: Where's the Inspector? I want to get out of here.
NAN: He's looking around. Thought the murderer might still be in here.
MEG: I've got a swell idea. Couldn't we wait for him outside?
NAN: I don't see why not. Let's get out of here. (They exit off. We hear rattling of door and the following dialogue offstage.) What's wrong?
TOM: The door is jammed.
JIMMY: Let me try. (They push, the door doesn't move) I thought these locked from the inside.
NAN: This has never happened before. Hey, someone has slipped a board through the handles. I see it through the crack. It's acting like a brace.
TOM: Buy why would anyone want to keep us in here. (INSPECTOR enters from opposite offstage area)
WEBB: Trying to make a break? (All enter)
NAN: We're locked in, Webb.
WEBB: What? (He exits off and hear him trying door) That's impossible.
TOM: Tell that to the murderer. Did you find him?

MURDER WELL REHEARSED

WEBB: No. (Enters) I looked all over after we found out that tape was a hoax. Someone is trying to make you look awfully guilty, Miss Benton. And he's doing a swell job.

NAN: Look, the light was set up to go off at a certain time along with that tape recording. I just happened to be in the spotlight, that's all.

WEBB: Well, whatever the reason, looks like we stay here until the other patrol cars arrive.

TOM: When will that be?

WEBB: Soon. They said as soon as they could. Once we get the body safely put away, you and I, Miss Benton, are going to have a little chat.

NAN: But I tell you . . .

WEBB: Say, where's the body? (They run up to where the body was. Pull away sheet. It is gone.) Someone did it during the blackout.

NAN: But who? And how did they get out if the doors were bolted?

TOM: The murderer probably slipped in, took the body and bolted the door when he left.

WEBB: How convenient for you, Benton. The body gone in a timed blackout.

NAN: Look, I was with you, remember? Then I came down here and the lights were on.

TOM: I felt a bump in the dark. As if someone was running past me.

WEBB: Which way was he running?

TOM: I couldn't tell. I was all mixed up in the dark.

WEBB: So, what we have is a murderer who was here until the blackout, he times the spot to hit Benton, grabs the body when everyone is confused, runs out and bolts the door.

NAN: So you think the murderer is gone.

WEBB: I think we're pretty safe, unless one of us happened to bolt the doors from the outside. (He sits on chair) We'll wait together and when the back-up units arrive, we'll search the theatre. Maybe he stashed the body somewhere. (Looks down on his pants) You theatre people really run a sloppy place.

NAN: Why?

WEBB: I got dirt or make-up on my pants. Look. (Brushes it away) Now, isn't this cozy. All of us waiting to be rescued by the police!

JIMMY: Hey, why don't we search this place ourselves. I don't like being sitting ducks for a killer.

NAN: But he must have left. The doors are bolted from the outside, remember? There's no way he could have gotten in.

SHEILA: And at least I feel a little safer.

JIMMY: Wait a minute. There is so a way he could have gotton in.

WEBB: How?

JIMMY: If what I think is true .... (He runs off. WEBB jumps up)

WEBB: Hey, come back here! You, Kid, come back ... (Runs after him)

MEG: What's up?

SHEILA: Jimmy must know something.

NAN: I hope the Inspector doesn't hurt him.

TOM: I don't like that guy. The funny thing is, he looks really familiar to me.

SHEILA: Too many murder rehearsals, Tom. All policemen in murder mysteries look the same. (WEBB re-enters with JIMMY in tow)

WEBB: You try that again, Kid, and you're in deep trouble.

JIMMY: But you don't get it.

NAN: What did you find, Jim?

JIMMY: I started thinking about being locked in and remembered a way out. The way I came in when I was locked out this evening.

TOM: The make-up room's broken window.

JIMMY: Yes. And look. (Holds up finger)

SHEILA: Blood?

JIMMY: Yes. I found it on the window sill. That's how it

got on my pants. When I crawled through the window!
NAN: That means . . . .
JIMMY: That the murderer killed Mr. Gleason somewhere else, then brought him here!
SHEILA: So the murder was committed before we arrived.
WEBB: Look, all this is just guessing. I think you've been rehearsing your murder mystery too much. Let me handle the detective work.
MEG: But why would someone want to put the body in here?
NAN: Better in here than in the middle of the football field.
WEBB: O.K., Sherlock Holmes. What makes you think the murder occurred on the football field? It could have been anywhere on school grounds.
NAN: Look. (She goes to sofa where body had been) Grass stains and a mixture of the chalk we use to mark the field. Either he was murdered on the field or nearby.
WEBB: Why didn't you mention this sooner?
NAN: I just realized.
MEG: But why did they put the body in here? There are a lot of other hiding places — like in one of the basketball players' lockers. They wouldn't have smelled Gleason for years!
NAN: The stage is close by. Besides, it was probably a frame-up.
ALL: Frame-up? What do you mean?
NAN: Sure. Someone knew Jimmy had an argument with Mr. Gleason. And they probably knew I was not in his favor. The murderer probably thought this would be the ideal place to drop the body off.
WEBB: Look, this is all a little too "pat". These historic discoveries just about the time I'm about to point out the murderer. They don't carry water. Especially since we don't have a body. Besides, anyone of you could have brought in those grass stains. Look, the wet grass sticks to your shoes. (He shows his own boot)
SHEILA: Yes, but . . .
TOM: Sheila, come here. (They begin to whisper)

MURDER WELL REHEARSED

NAN: Let's climb out the window and wait for the ambulance outside. (TOM and SHEILA sneak off)

WEBB: (Frantic) No! Absolutely not! We should search this place first.

NAN: Surely you don't want to put our lives in jeopardy, do you?

WEBB: Of course not. You're in no danger. But I think we should make a search of the . . . Hey! Where are those other kids?

JIMMY: (Looks around) Tom and Sheila are gone!

WEBB: Find them! I don't want them snooping around by themselves. (Jumps from stage in search of TOM and SHEILA)

NAN: (Shouting) Sheila! Tom!

MEG: They're probably hiding.

JIMMY: That's not like them. (They start to search. MEG opens the closet door on stage and the body falls out)

MEG: (Screaming) I found Mr. Gleason!

NAN: (Running to the body) But . . . but why did . . . why in there?

WEBB: (Jumps back on stage) Look, don't touch that! Find those kids and . . . (We hear an ambulance siren off) What's that?

NAN: Probably the ambulance you called for.

MEG: Sounds more like the police.

WEBB: Did you call them?

NAN: No. You did. I tried but the phone wasn't working. The switchboard was dead . . . (Suddenly realizing) Say, how could you have called the hospital if the phone wasn't working?

WEBB: I . . . I didn't call them from here. I tried to, but like you said, the phones didn't work. I . . . I called at the precinct.

JIMMY: If you had called from the station, they would have come with you.

WEBB: No . . . not really, you see . . . (Siren gets louder) Hey let's get out of here and wait somewhere else.

MURDER WELL REHEARSED   Page 20

JIMMY: We'd better wait for the cops.

WEBB: Look, I'm running this show. I say we wait outside.

NAN: You seem really nervous at the prospect of facing some of your own co-workers. Maybe we'd better get a better look at your identification.

WEBB: What? You don't suspect me, do you?

NAN: Look, all I want to do is . . . (WEBB draws gun. MEG screams)

WEBB: O.K., now you know. I'm no policeman. But I got to get out of here before the real cops get here. (He starts exiting towards auditorium and is in front of the curtain line when curtain suddenly closes, separating him from the rest of the cast.) Hey! What's going on! (The lights go off except for a spotlight centered directly on him. He whirls around, pointing the gun at the spotlight) I can't see. I'll shoot! (Shoots blindly toward the light. NAN and JIMMY enter from under curtain and both grab at the gun, they wrestle in the light, then fall into the darkness. We hear the fight and when the spotlight finds them again, NAN and JIMMY are standing over the knocked out WEBB.)

NAN: Kill the light. (The spot goes off as the other lights come up. MEG peeks head through curtain.)

MEG: What happened? (Enters full)

NAN: We caught ourselves a murderer.

JIMMY: But why would an inspector want to kill Gleason?

NAN: Look closely. (They lean over as she takes off the glasses and moustache and hat of WEBB. It is really Frank.)

JIMMY: It's Frank!

NAN: Right. Somehow, he tripped himself up . . . (TOM enters from back of auditorium.)

TOM: Correction. We tripped him up.

NAN: Tom, where's Sheila?

TOM: Getting the police. Those sirens you heard were just sound effect records. You see, we suspected this guy for a long time. (Onto stage)

MEG: What tipped you?

TOM: Look at his coat. I wore that in "Our Town" last year. See where I ripped it during dress rehearsal?
NAN: That made you think he was the murderer?
TOM: No not really. When I recognized the coat, I thought it was funny that an inspector would wear a costume. Then I figured he was the murderer coming back for something. When he said the ambulance was on its way and I knew the phones were out, I figured he was trying to keep this from getting out until he could get whatever he came for. Besides, it doesn't make sense that one policeman would be assigned to a murder case.
NAN: So, he murdered Mr. Gleason, dragged the body here to confuse the cops and tried to put the blame on one of us.
JIMMY: He was still here when I came, so whammo! I get it in the head.
MEG: Then he hightailed it to the costume department ...
NAN: No. First he went home, so I could find him in to let me in the theatre. Jimmy, open the curtain, will ya? (JIMMY exits.)
MEG: Then to the costume department for a change of identity. But why didn't he just leave and call the police? All the clues to blame us were planted. (Curtain opens, JIMMY enters. All cross onto main acting area.)
TOM: Elementary, my dear girl. I figured that he was not done with the body. Evidently, the body held something that could point the finger at him. So during the blackout that he himself rigged while pretending to use the phone, I ran to the body and hid it in the closet. I also found these. (Shows newspaper clippings.)
NAN: Newspaper clippings. (Reading) "Joseph Berg released from prison." (MEG looks over shoulder)
MEG: Why, the picture is of Frank.
NAN: So Frank was in prison. (FRANK starts to recover)
FRANK: What happened? (NAN holds gun, rushing to him)
TOM: We know everything!
FRANK: (Slowly getting up, he sees clippings) You found the

MURDER WELL REHEARSED

clippings. So you know that I was in prison.

NAN: We know that, but why did you murder Mr. Gleason?

FRANK: Gleason found those clippings and threatened to tell the authorities. I needed this job. He was blackmailing me.

MEG: So this whole thing was done so you could get the clippings off the body.

JIMMY: But how could you have put the boards through the door handles if you were in here with us?

FRANK: Same way you got in and out. During the blackout I climbed through the make-up room's window and bolted the doors. (Sirens are heard)

NAN: Is that the record?

FRANK: Record? You mean I was caught with my own trick?

NAN: Right. All that knowledge of how the light timer and tape recorder works should have tipped us off that whoever the Inspector really was, he had a lot of know-how about this place. (They listen for siren)

TOM: That's the real police. I sent Sheila to call them.

NAN: Well, Tom, you really rehearsed well for your part.

MEG: This is one rehearsal I won't forget.

NAN: Jimmy, you jump out the window and unbolt the door. I know a few people who are waiting for your debut, Frank. The police for one. (JIMMY exits)

MEG: This is almost as good as our own play. (They start to exit.) Miss Benton?

NAN: Yes, Meg?

MEG: Next year, could we do a musical? I mean something light and fun, no dead bodies, no unexpected lighting effects and no hysterics. I'm sick of murder mysteries!
(All laugh and the sirens get louder. Lights fade, curtain closes as all start to exit, laughing.)

CURTAIN FALLS

PRODUCTION NOTES

Upon reading, it will become quite obvious that MURDER WELL REHEARSED is meant to be played as a thriller. A number of suggestions are hereby indicated in order to gain the effect the playwright intended. FRANK should be played in hidden light and blocked in such a manner that the audience never gets a good glimpse of him. THE INSPECTOR, on the other hand — because of the dual role must completely overshadow the resemblance to FRANK. Thus, when true identity is revealed, the moment becomes a tense and exciting shock. The role of FRANK should either not be given billing or a fictitious name substituted. Members of the cast should not reveal to anyone the nature of the dual role. The blackouts must be carefully timed and much improvised dialogue should be introduced to heighten tension during said blackouts. MEG introduces some comedy relief in the drama and should be played in an open, honest manner. NAN can easily be changed to a man's role.

www.ingramcontent.com/pod-product-compliance
Lightning Source LLC
Chambersburg PA
CBHW071848290426
44109CB00017B/1967